OXOX

Hugs & Kisses

INTRODUCTION BY Mimi Coucher

A TINY FOLIO™
ABBEVILLE PRESS PUBLISHERS
NEW YORK LONDON PARIS

Front cover: Detail of Elizabeth Taylor and Montgomery Clift, from *A Place in the Sun*, 1951. See page 136.

Back cover: Sonja Bullaty, date unknown.

Frontispiece: Detail of Ernst Haas, New York, 1958. See page 117.

Page 6: Detail of Elliott Erwitt, California, 1955. See page 115.

Page 9: Henri Cartier-Bresson, Dieppe, France, 1929.

Page 12: Costa Manos, 1958.

Page 15: Julie Christie and Omar Sharif, from *Dr. Zhivago*, 1965.

Pages 16–17: Detail of photographer unknown, Paris, 1952.

Pages 92–93: Detail of photographer unknown, Paris, 1950.

Pages 166–67: Detail of Burt Glinn, 1961.

Pages 228–29: Detail of Danny Lyon, 1985.

For Cataloging-in-Publication Data, see page 286.

Contents

Introduction

by Mimi Coucher

Each of us has a secret camera. It sits, invisible, in the eye, recording the intimate moments of our lives and storing them in our very private galleries. We keep these images sacred, turning to them in times of love, joy, sorrow, and when in need of a dose of misty nostalgia.

There are also secret cameras outside ourselves. Small, black, and mechanical, these cameras click and whir under the push of strangers' fingers. Peering through lenses, artists' eyes have found fleeting moments when emotions could be captured and kept. The resulting photographs— whispery or bold, crisp or crackled, intense or sentimental—can so move us that they become permanently fixed in our minds, and part of our emotional history.

Photographs, like our own memories, transcend time and dissolve cultural boundaries. . . . A dark-eyed woman gazes at her dance partner at Queen Charlotte's Ball in 1967; the following year, a young man with a half-burned cig in his mouth makes a peace sign at the Democratic National Convention. Culturally, the two are worlds apart—she in her fur-trimmed ball gown, he in his ripped jeans—but the look in their eyes is the same. Her passionate gaze belies her careful hair; his casual gesture of "peace" reads more like "V for Victory," his other arm draped around a woman snuggled into his shoulder. . . .

Two pairs of legs protrude from underneath a black umbrella on a beach in France. It is 1929, but the moment is barely different from the one shared between a wounded soldier and his lover in a Tel Aviv hospital in 1967, or that of an entranced Parisian couple who keep a waiter waiting at a sidewalk café in 1958. For more than a hundred years, cameras have captured intimate moments between lovers, yet even the most antiquated images remain as fresh as a spring romance. Whether photographed on a subway platform, or in a shiny new automobile parked at the edge of the ocean, or in the blessed darkness of a movie theater, it is the moment of human contact that resonates. All else is atmosphere, props, passing scenery.

Our culture is kind to lovers; we see these photographs and think of romance, sweet love, happy endings. But in other times and other places, kissing was a private act too powerful to be practiced in public. In ancient China, kissing and embracing were serious areas of study. If performed properly and under the correct circumstances, intimate touch would, it is told, unfold a thousand charms and erase a hundred sorrows. But never in public. In China, street displays of affection were for harlots and sinners, not those engaged in the holy art of love.

In our liberal society, the details of celebrities' personal lives can be witnessed on TV and in tabloids every day. And yet there is still something thrilling about glimpsing strangers kissing on the sidewalk, or clinging to one another while walking through the park. We may be immune to lurid particulars snapped by paparazzi, but innocent images caught by discreet cameras still have the power to warm us. Did the couple who stood knee-deep in the sparkling

waters of Palermo know they were being photographed? It doesn't seem possible: their stance is too candid and supercharged with emotion. Perhaps it is love, more than sex, that truly has the power to make us blush. . . .

You may kiss the bride. Upon that kiss pivots the future and the past. The papers have been signed; the rings have been exchanged; the parents have been appeased and have, in their secret hearts, surrendered; the friends have teased and tormented and celebrated in that way that friends have of saying good-bye; but it is the kiss that makes it official. Now you can legally be left alone, you and your love.

But first, glasses will ring with the sound of a hundred spoons begging you to kiss. Photographers will straddle the backseats of limousines and coax you. As you pull away from the rice-throwing throngs, cans and shoes will rattle on the street and horns from strangers' cars will honk and honk, but all the noise will not drown out the sound in your own head that says, I am delivered.

Toddlers are sweetly prodded, amid flashbulb-lit birthday parties and holiday gatherings, in kitchens festooned with crepe paper and paper plates, to kiss aunts, uncles, cousins, baby-sitters. There is no pull to those baby kisses;

the wet mouth of the child is laid for a second upon the dry cheek of the adult. And yet, for all the passivity of the kiss, some bloom springs forth: the grown-up remembers why work is worth doing well, why sacrifices are made.

Baby kisses, limp and damp, connect the future to the past. Baby kisses give new eyes to weary adults. With baby kisses, battle scars are softened.

Witness a mother hugging her child: who is comforting whom? The child, floppy and thinking of candy, endures the embrace. The mother, knowing the dangers of strangers and pain, hopes to imprint the child with her own fearless love, wants the whole world to know that her child is protected, even when alone. How many mothers wish they could enclose their half-helpless offspring in their own knowing skin? The hug is the best they can do; it is the only physical way they have of infusing their precious children with the strength to survive.

"That is not a kiss," thinks the petulant teenager, seeing her grandfather place a chaste peck on the face of her grandma.

Oh, but it is. With that schoolboyish kiss is an adoring recognition of all that has come before, of all the qualities that age cannot diminish, and a celebration of the quiet, winking triumph of having survived. It's a kiss of gratitude for a lifetime shared. Or maybe it's just a spontaneous burst of affection.

The impulsiveness of that kiss is mirrored, across the age divide, by the effortless hugs and kisses of children unburdened by anxiety or doubt. They'll snuggle puppies, chase after kittens, throw their arms around a big brother or sister, plant a kiss on an infant's face, or climb on the lap of someone who, on their child radar, has registered as "friend."

With age, such spontaneous lovebursts fade; they are slowly replaced by a creeping possessiveness of personal space, a taste for privacy that makes old friends all the more precious.

Look at the photo of two old men embracing in a Paris bistro. Notice their angular shoes, their worn trench coats, their thick hands clutching unfiltered cigarettes and each other. They hug with their eyes squeezed shut, feeling the bond of years, speaking and listening all at once, without language. What more could you want from this life than a person who, as the old saw goes, knows everything about you but loves you anyway? True friendship is almost too much to ask for. Unmuddied by mutual attraction, or hormones, or agendas, friendships are what we count on to get us through the best times, the worst times, the dull times, the tragic times.

And when humans aren't available, dogs come to our emotional rescue. They are the empaths of the animal world, they seem to intuit exactly when we're at our lowest. It is then that they'll come trotting quietly to our side, give us a lick, and lie at our feet. Dogs (and even cats sometimes) are the champions of listening, always ready to offer peaceful companionship and unconditional love.

Have you ever loved someone who doesn't even know that you exist? Sure you have. That's the thrill of movies.

Hollywood makes kisses bigger than kisses have ever been before. We not only witness the moment of contact, we enter into emotional complexities that loom nearly as large as those in our own love lives. Sitting in the dark, absorbed by a story, our hearts hanging on words and gestures, we become the rough, the tender, the brave, the beautiful one whose lips are the messengers of what lies mute in our hearts.

In movies, passion never fades. Rhett consumes the ravishing Scarlett; her cheeks are as fine and her lips are as red, his back is as broad and his grin as rakish, as they were in 1939, as they will be in 2010. Will the blue ever drain from the Hustler's eyes? Will curvy women with strippers' names ever be able to resist James Bond's smooth seductions?

We look, we learn, we linger. Movies become a touch-stone for our own lives: at fifteen we laugh at the stagy antics of the "old people"; at thirty we marvel at their Technicolor beauty; at forty-five we notice how young the cinematic lovers seem. We cluck with fond indul-gence at their innocent intimacies, thinking of our sons' and daughters' urgent energies, thinking of our own florid youthfulness.

You must remember this: a kiss isn't just a kiss. There are smooches, busses, pecks, smacks, lip locks, first kisses, last kisses, kisses of death, kisses of life, soul kisses, air kisses, French kisses, butterfly kisses, lipstick kisses, good-bye kisses. Each carries with it a story as deep and unique as a face or a fingerprint.

Frozen in time, the photos remind us. They come to us in black and white, these images of strangers' intimacies in doorways and cars and bedrooms and kitchens and alleys and fields and altars. We fill in the colors, drawing upon the palettes of our private passions, remembering the brilliant, soft, cool details of the things we have done, the things we've wished we'd done, the things we may do yet.

In the days of early Christianity, documents were signed with an *X*. This symbolized the Calvary cross, and also referred to *Xristos*, the Greek word for Christ. Once the mark was made, the signer would seal his sworn oath with a kiss. An *O* isn't just a letter in the alphabet: it is a symbol of eternity, an encirclement without beginning or end. It represents a hug, an embrace of affection and protection. So when we sign our letters with *XX*s and *OO*s, we make a promise: we swear to keep our beloved safe within a circle of love.

Calling
All
Lovers!

Louis Stettner, Paris, 1950.

Photographer unknown, 1953.

Photographer unknown, Paris, 1951.

Henri Cartier-Bresson, Paris, 1958.

OX
XO

Elliott Erwitt, Paris, 1970.

ALL
LOVERS!

Henri Cartier-Bresson, Paris, 1953.

Marc Riboud, 1953.

Josef Koudelka, Venice, Italy, 1997.

OX
XO

Debbie Fleming Caffrey, Lisbon, Portugal, 1990.

Eric Kroll, Canton, China, 1990.

Thomas Hoepker,
New York, 1990.

Henri Cartier-Bresson, France, 1936.

Elliott Erwitt, Paris, 1966.

OX
XO

Gilles Peress, 1973.

Larry Towell, 1992.

Leonard Freed, 1964.

P. J. Griffiths, 1995.

OX
XO

Bruce Davidson, New York, 1992.

Bruce Davidson, New York, 1992.

O✗
✗O

Eugene Richards, San Antonio, Texas, 1995.

Bruce Davidson, New York, 1966.

OX
XO

Ferdinando Scianna, New York, 1985.

Martine Franck, Budapest, date unknown.

OX
XO

Bruce Davidson, New York, 1995.

Elliott Erwitt, 1962.

O✗
✗O

Elliott Erwitt, Miami Beach, 1993.

Sylvia Plachy, New York, 1994.

Elliott Erwitt, Mexico, 1973.

Bruce Davidson, New York, 1959.

OX
XO

Larry Silver, 1990.

Dennis Stock, date unknown.

o✗
✗o

Bruce Davidson, 1958.

Jack Gorman, San Francisco, 1951.

O✗
✗O

Eugene Richards, 1983.

Cornell Capa, Tel Aviv, Israel, 1967.

H. Armstrong Roberts, Philadelphia, 1940.

H. Armstrong Roberts, Philadelphia, 1977.

OX
XO

H. Armstrong Roberts, Philadelphia, 1969.

Burt Glinn, Fire Island, New York, 1961.

O X
X O

Burt Glinn, Chicago, 1968.

Hiroji Kubota, Laguna Beach, California, date unknown.

Wayne Miller, Berkeley, California, 1965.

Roger Malloch, Chicago, 1960.

O X
X O

Richard Kalvar, New York, date unknown.

Stephan Zaubitzer, Paris, 1992.

o X
X O

Erich Hartmann, Italy, 1988.

OX
XO

Sylvia Plachy, Virginia, 1979 (detail).

Sylvia Plachy, Brooklyn, 1986.

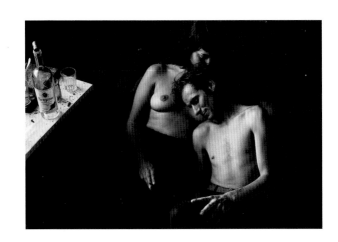

Ed Van der Elsken, Paris, 1950-54.

Costa Manos, Berlin, 1965.

OX
XO

Photographer unknown, London, 1949.

OX
XO

Danny Lyon, New York, 1992.

Bruce Davidson, New York, 1959.

OX
XO

P. J. Griffiths, date unknown.

Stephan Zaubitzer, London, 1995.

OX
XO

Henri Cartier-Bresson, 1950s.

Peter Hunter, London, 1939.

David Hurn, England, 1967.

Ed Van der Wijk, The Hague, c. 1955.

David Hurn, date unknown.

David Hurn, date unknown.

OX
XO

Photographer unknown, Queens, New York, date unknown.

Camerique, New York (?), 1938.

OX
XO

Keri Pickett, Minneapolis, 1991.

Erich Hartmann, Troy, New York, c. 1950.

Cornell Capa, 1962.

Elliott Erwitt, date unknown.

Henri Cartier-Bresson, New York, 1959.

Eli Reed, Atlanta, Georgia, 1993.

O X
X O

Inge Morath, New York, 1960.

Dennis Stock, Paris, 1958.

Henri Cartier-Bresson, Paris, 1969.

Abbas, Paris, 1973.

OX
XO

96

Erich Hartmann,
Paris, 1973.

OX
XO

Thomas Hoepker, 1978.

Genevieve Naylor, Paris, 1953.

OX
XO

Raymond Depardon, Paris, 1988.

Erich Hartmann, Paris, 1975.

OX
XO

Louis Stettner, Holland, c. 1959.

Bruce Davidson, New York, 1960.

Micha Bar'Am, Jerusalem, date unknown.

Frank Horvat, Paris, 1956.

OX
XO

Josef Koudelka, Lourdes, France, 1973.

Henri Cartier-Bresson, Paris, 1959.

Josef Koudelka, Czechoslovakia, date unknown.

Ed Van der Elsken, Paris, 1950–54.

OX
XO

Guy Le Querrèc, Paris, 1979.

Ian Berry, date unknown.

OX
XO

Bruce Davidson, New York, 1995.

Sylvia Plachy, New York, 1996.

o X
X O

Elliott Erwitt, California, 1955.

o✗
✗o

Ernst Haas, New York, 1958.

OX
XO

Dennis Stock, 1952.

Elliott Erwitt, Valencia, Spain, 1952.

OX
XO

Henri Cartier-Bresson,
Newcastle, England, 1978.

OX
XO

Camerique, California, c. 1940s.

Keri Pickett, Kawashaway Radical Faerie Sanctuary, 1995.

124

Guy Hersant, Paris, 1996.

O X
X O

Wayne Miller, San Francisco, 1957.

Alfred Eisenstaedt, New York, 1945.

OX
XO

Photographer unknown, Waterloo Station, London, 1939.

Camerique, New Hope, Pennsylvania, 1941–45.

OX
XO

Photographer unknown, 1938.

Photographer unknown, 1970s.

OX
XO

Warren Beatty and Natalie Wood, *Splendor in the Grass*, 1961.

George Peppard and Audrey Hepburn, *Breakfast at Tiffany's*, 1961.

OX
XO

Tom Ewell and Marilyn Monroe, *Seven Year Itch*, 1957.

Burt Lancaster and Deborah Kerr, *From Here to Eternity*, 1953.

OX
XO

Elizabeth Taylor and Montgomery Clift, *A Place in the Sun,* 1951.

Stefania Sandrelli and Jean-Louis Trintignant, *The Conformist*, 1971.

OX
XO

Photographer unknown, English Channel, 1962.

Photographer unknown, Trafalgar Square, London, 1969.

OX
XO

Roger Malloch, Chicago, 1960.

Photographer unknown, Isle of Wight, England, 1970.

H. Armstrong Roberts, Philadelphia, 1960.

Photographer unknown, 1980.

Ferdinando Scianna, New York, 1985.

Bruce Davidson, New York, 1959.

OX
XO

Bruce Davidson, New York, 1959.

Bruce Davidson, New York, 1959.

o x
x o

Allan Grant, c. 1950.

Franco Zecchin, Palermo, Italy, 1987.

Elliott Erwitt, New York, 1955.

Burt Glinn, New York, 1950s.

OX
XO

Bruce Davidson,
New York, 1995.

OX
XO

Karen Hirshan, Santa Monica, California, 1994.

Andrea Sperling, New York, 1996.

O X
X O

Photographer unknown, Chicago, 1948.

Mary Ann Jackson and "Wheezer," from *Our Gang*, 1935.

OX
XO

Photographer unknown, London, 1926.

Photographer unknown, Victoria, Australia, 1946.

o X
X O

Andrea Modica, Treadwell, New York, 1987.

Joseph Koudelka, date unknown.

OX
XO

Elliott Erwitt, New York, 1955.

Henri Cartier-Bresson, Germany, 1960.

Elliott Erwitt, Kraków, Poland, 1964.

Sabine Weiss, Paris, c. 1949.

Love Under the Lights

OX
XO

Rudolph Valentino and Vilma Banky, *The Son of the Sheik*, 1926.

Greta Garbo and John Gilbert, *Flesh and the Devil*, 1926.

Arletty and Jean-Louis Barrault, *Children of Paradise*, 1944.

Gloria Swanson and Walter Byron, *Queen Kelly*, 1927.

o ✗
✗ o

Helen Hayes
and Gary Cooper,
A Farewell to Arms, 1932.

OX
XO

Greta Garbo and Robert Taylor, *Camille*, 1936.

John Boles and Bebe Daniels, *Rio Rita*, 1929.

Katharine Hepburn and James Stewart, *The Philadelphia Story*, 1940.

OX
XO

John Howard and Katharine Hepburn,
The Philadelphia Story, 1940.

Ginger Rogers and Fred Astaire, *Swing Time*, 1936.

Leslie Howard and Vivien Leigh, *Gone with the Wind*, 1939.

Clark Gable and Vivien Leigh, *Gone with the Wind,* 1939.

OX
XO

Clark Gable and Vivien Leigh, *Gone with the Wind*, 1939.

Vivien Leigh and Clark Gable, *Gone with the Wind,* 1939.

OX
XO

Donna Reed, James Stewart, et al.,
It's a Wonderful Life, 1946.

Gary Cooper and Patricia Neal, *The Fountainhead*, 1949.

Glenn Ford and Rita Hayworth, *Gilda*, 1946.

OX
XO

Ingrid Bergman and Gary Cooper, *For Whom the Bell Tolls*, 1943.

Gary Cooper and Ingrid Bergman, *For Whom the Bell Tolls*, 1943.

OX
XO

Ingrid Bergman and Humphrey Bogart, *Casablanca*, 1942.

Lauren Becall and Humphrey Bogart, *To Have and Have Not*, 1944.

O X
X O

Rita Hayworth and Glenn Ford, *Gilda*, 1946.

Orson Welles and Rita Hayworth, *Lady from Shanghai,* 1948.

OX
XO

Bing Crosby and Grace Kelly, *High Society*, 1956.

Bing Crosby, John Lund, Grace Kelly, and Frank Sinatra,
High Society, 1956.

OX
XO

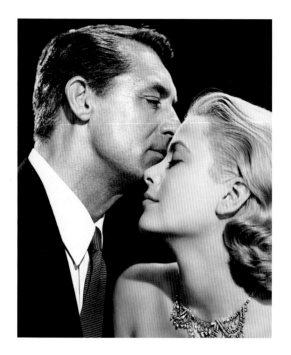

Cary Grant and Grace Kelly, *To Catch a Thief*, 1955.

Elizabeth Taylor and Rock Hudson, *Giant*, 1956.

Cary Grant and Eva Marie Saint, *North by Northwest*, 1959.

Kim Novak and James Stewart, *Vertigo*, 1958.

OX
XO

Tommy Noonan and Marilyn Monroe, *Gentlemen Prefer Blondes*, 1953.

Clark Gable and Marilyn Monroe, *The Misfits*, 1961.

OX
XO

Marilyn Monroe and Clark Gable,
The Misfits, 1961.

Humphrey Bogart and Audrey Hepburn, *Sabrina*, 1954.

Dorothy Dandridge and Harry Belafonte, *Carmen Jones*, 1954.

OX
XO

Kirk Douglas and Kim Novak, *Strangers When We Meet*, 1960.

Piper Laurie and Paul Newman, *The Hustler*, 1961.

Sophia Lauren and Marcello Mastroianni,
Yesterday, Today and Tomorrow, 1964.

Sophia Lauren, Marcello Mastroianni, et al.,
Yesterday, Today and Tomorrow, 1964.

OX
XO

John Kerr and Norma Crane, *Tea and Sympathy*, 1959.

Warren Beatty and Natalie Wood, *Splendor in the Grass,* 1961.

Jeanne Moreau and Alain Cuny, *The Lovers*, 1958.

William Holden and Jennifer Jones, *Love Is a Many-Splendored Thing*, 1955.

213

OX
XO

Anna Karina and Jean-Paul Belmondo, *Pierrot le Fou*, 1965.

Julie Christie and Omar Sharif, *Dr. Zhivago*, 1965.

OX
XO

Sean Connery and Daniela Bianchi, *From Russia with Love*, 1963.

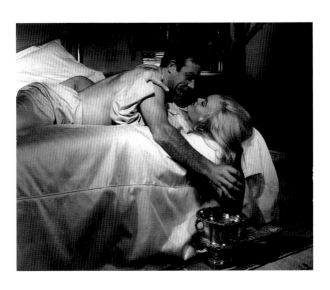

Sean Connery and Shirley Eaton, *Goldfinger,* 1964.

OX
XO

Faye Dunaway and Warren Beatty, *Bonnie and Clyde*, 1967.

Faye Dunaway and Jack Nicholson, *Chinatown*, 1974.

OX
XO

Robert Redford and Mia Farrow, *The Great Gatsby*, 1974.

Perry King and Raquel Welch, *The Wild Party*, 1975.

o✗
✗o

Diane Keaton and Woody Allen,
Manhattan, 1979.

OX
XO

Richard Gere and Lauren Hutton, *American Gigolo*, 1980.

Eiko Matsuda and Tatsuya Fuji, *In the Realm of the Senses,* 1976.

OX
XO

Rae Dawn Chong and Bennet Guillory, *The Color Purple*, 1985.

Drew Barrymore and E.T., *E.T.—The Extra-Terrestrial,* 1982.

Friends & Family

Leonard Freed, New York, 1963.

Sylvia Plachy, New York, 1982.

OX
XO

Sylvia Plachy, New York, 1989.

Sylvia Plachy, New York, c. 1978.

Costa Manos, U.S.S.R., 1965.

Josef Koudelka, Moscow, 1989.

OX
XO

Elliott Erwitt, New York, 1977.

O X
X O

Sylvia Plachy, 1995.

Barbara Comnes, Nevada, 1992.

OX
XO

Elliott Erwitt, 1995.

Hiroji Kubota, Inverness, California, 1971.

o X
X O

Barbara Comnes, San Anselmo, California, 1996.

Hiroji Kubota, New York, 1966.

OX
XO

Laura Straus, New York, 1996.

Frances M. Cox, Pennsylvania (?), c. 1985.

Mark J. Goebel, 1993.

Barbara Comnes, San Anselmo, California, 1995.

Eve Arnold, U.S.S.R., 1966.

Photographer unknown, 1965.

OX
XO

Andrea Modica, Colorado Springs, 1994.

Sonja Bullaty, c. 1950s.

O X
X O

Josef Koudelka, London, date unknown.

Photographer unknown, 1954.

Richard Kalvar, Paris, 1965.

Keri Pickett, Minneapolis, 1992.

OX
XO

Ian Berry, between East and West Berlin, 1963.

Josef Koudelka, Spain, date unknown.

Louis Stettner, Provincetown, Massachusetts, c. 1954.

Elliott Erwitt, 1954.

OX
XO

Erich Hartmann, New York, 1956.

Robert Capa, Paris, 1936.

OX
XO

Guy Le Querrèc, France, 1978.

Leonard Freed, 1963.

OX
XO

Danny Lyon, 1988.

Eugene Richards, Alpha, Oregon, 1991.

Leonard Freed, Chapel Hill, North Carolina, date unknown.

Karen Tweedy-Holmes, New York, 1992.

Karen Tweedy-Holmes, Columbus, Ohio, 1980.

Doris Ulmann, North Carolina, c. 1933.

o✗
✗o

Guy Hersant, 1983.

Erich Hartmann, Italy, c.1984.

OX
XO

Barbara Comnes, San Anselmo, California, date unknown.

Sally Mann, Lexington, Virginia, 1988.

o X
X O

Josef Koudelka,
near Naples, Italy,
date unknown.

OX
XO

Jean Gaumy, date unknown.

Gilles Peress, 1976.

Sonja Bullaty, c. 1950s.

Elliott Erwitt, date unknown.

OX
XO

Magnum, date unknown.

Susan Meiselas, date unknown.

O X
X O

Eugene Richards, Brooklyn, New York, 1988.

Eugene Richards, near Albuquerque, New Mexico, 1990.

Photography Credits

EDITOR: Jeffrey Golick
DESIGNER: Celia Fuller
PICTURE EDITORS: Naomi Ben-Shahar,
Elizabeth Boyle, and Laura Straus
PRODUCTION MANAGER: Elizabeth Gaynor

First edition
10 9 8 7 6 5 4 3 2 1

Library of Congress Cataloging-in-Publication Data

Hugs & kisses / introduction by Mimi Coucher. — 1st ed.
p. cm.
"A tiny folio."
ISBN 0-7892-0427-4
1. Hugging.   2. Kissing.   1. Coucher, Mimi.
BF637.H83H84   1998
306. 7—dc21   97-32509

About the Author

O X O X

Mimi Coucher writes about
food, fashion, life, and love,
including sex and love quizzes
for *Cosmopolitan*.

Tiny Folios™ available from Abbeville Press